Desert Plant Personalities

Dry Humor on the Caliche

A Sonoran Desert Plant Family Album

Photos and text by
Morris Lundin

MORI STUDIO SOUTHWEST
Fountain Hills, Arizona

Copyright © 2000 by Morris Lundin

All rights reserved. No part of this work may be reproduced in any manner without verbal or written permission of the author. Reviewers may quote excerpts or reproduce photos for publication in a positive review.

ISBN 0-9679349-0-7

Printed in the United States of America

10   9   8   7   6   5   4   3   2   1

Order more copies from:

Mori Studio Southwest
P.O Box 18547
Fountain Hills, AZ 85269-8547

Queries:

Phone: 480-816-4407
E-mail: morisota@aol.com

Contents

Jolly Chollas 1

True Frondship: The Palm Branch of the Family 5

Perky but Prickly: Cactus Lowlife 17

The Stately, Salacious, Shy Saguaros 23

Preface

As a child growing up on the flat, grassy plains of northern Minnesota, I spent countless minutes (short attention span) lying on the fragrant grass of a newly-mowed lawn looking up at billowing cumulus clouds. The swirling vapors evolved and dissolved as expressive human faces or wandering animals in the imaginative depths of a child's mind.

Years rolled on like the thunderheads after a storm and I found in myself the stirrings of a second childhood and the desire to turn to the clouds again to rekindle my imagination. However, after a few minutes of lying on my back on rocky desert caliche soil, staring at the deep blue cloudless Arizona sky, I realized that inspiration from above might be long in coming. I sat up, dusted myself off and became aware of a nearby saguaro silently staring at this snowbird as if to say, "I may not have seen much snow, but I know a flake when I see one!" Thus began an affinity for desert vegetation...since I am a transplant myself!

Conversing with native Arizonans and reading literature about the Sonoran desert made me realize I was not the first person to imagine giant saguaros imitating human forms. Soon the saguaros were joined by cholla, prickly pear and palms as their various shapes took on human characteristics in my mind.

For several years, an array of sophisticated photographic equipment—actually an automatic snapshot camera that fit in my pocket—accompanied me on drives, bicycle rides and hikes in and around Fountain Hills. Many of the spiny and frondy friends portrayed in this booklet still stand patiently observing the daily rush of citizens and visitors through the Valley. A few of the plants have since succumbed to development or age and deterioration.

This small album is an attempt to stimulate the reader's imagination and to help me remember some of the characters on the caliche.

To Our Readers

Caliche *(ka-leech'-ee)* is defined as a hard, crusty, whitish rock made up of calcium carbonate and other minerals mixed with gravel in arid soil. Anyone who has tried to plant a tree or dig a trench in caliche may add to the description.

The plants in this book were photographed in their natural state. In a few cases, non-essential background items have been removed. No express written consent was obtained from the plants photographed.

The names given to the plant characters portrayed herein are purely fictitious and any resemblance to plants you may have named yourself is purely coincidental.

Jolly Chollas

Inquisitive, a city slicker
Was unaware of cholla stickers.
    He gave a teddy bear a hug.
    You knew from horror on his mug
That nothing could have taught him quicker.

Aunt Cholly was proud of her new coiffure...

...until she realized several of her cronies had been to the same hairdresser!

The Cholla cousins have been greatly influenced by their favorite television program—"Touched by an Angel".

True Frondship: The Palm Branch of the Family

To plant a palm, I cogitate:
"A coco? Date?" I vacillate.
    If I should stand beneath the tree
    When fruit succumbs to gravity,
The wiser choice would be a date.

Granny Coco was the true matriarch of the Palm branch of the family.

Grandpa Coco sometimes showed the strain of living forty years with Granny.

Dato Palm, with his Afro, beard and necklace, never quite let go of his days as a hippie.

Dato's kids were more into punk.

Palmyra's skin problem seems to be clearing up nicely. Everyone wanted to know the name of her dermatologist.

Some of Palmyra's friends had good luck with their complexions, too, but with opposite results.

Three of the Palm boys tried unsuccesfully to suck in their bellies ...

...to impress the lovely Frond sisters who live across the street.

The Palm family welcomed the maestro himself, arriving to conduct a session of "Sing-a-long with Mitch."

The Three Wise Men in the Christmas pageant as played by the Palm triplets. Anyone remember the frankincense?

Several of the Palms decided they needed to slim down a little. Here they are getting ready to exercise to a Richard Simmons workout video.

Perky but Prickly: Cactus Lowlife

If common salad greens you waive;
And prickly pear is what you crave.
　Take care in culinary prep.
　Should you forget a simple step,
You'll think your salad needs a shave.

Ferdy Flatleaf shows off souvenir headgear he got on a recent trip to Disney World.

The Flatleaf twins were mischief-makers. They were always getting under somebody's skin. They truly were a prickly pair.

Cousin Pere stumped everyone at charades. Some of the guesses were: "Prince Charles", "Ross Perot" or "Dumbo".

Flora Flatleaf was always straining to pick up the latest gossip among the prickly pears.

Franky Flatleaf wandered off the trail into a patch of quicksand. Anybody got a rope?

The Stately, Salacious, Shy Saguaros

Once I saw a desert plant
Growing quite recalcitrant;
   A cactus tall
    With spines and all,
Its arms a bit protuberant.

Stretch Saguaro shared his dream of becoming an NBA star with two his younger cousins.

Beanpole's basketball career was put on hold when he dislocated his right shoulder.

Seems cousin Spike had a little run-in with the law. After a few minutes of hiding in the bushes, he was persuaded to give himself up.

Sally Saguaro models her tutu after recently being chosen lead dancer in the local ballet.

Cousin Cactusflower and her new boyfriend were almost inseparable. Shall we dance?

"I solemnly swear to uphold my duties as King...."

Sandy and Cindy Saguaro surveying the site of their new dream home.

Garo Saguaro never tired of telling everyone of his glory days as an NFL referee.

While reliving the days when he sailed with Captain Nemo, Uncle Salty often demonstrated the time he had to wrestle a giant octopus.

The Samson Saguaro balancing act was a hit with the Ringling Brothers circus crowds. But Uncle Samson, worn out from anchoring the pyramid, says next time he'd try the trapeze.

Showing some nervousness before speaking at the annual Save the Desert banquet, Stan Saguaro developed a severe case of hiccups.

The family chose up sides for the traditional pick-up softball game. Slugger Saguaro was first up to bat.

The Barrel twins, Bobby and Bubba, loved to play outlaws hiding in the rocks.

Slim was always ready and willing to demonstrate his quick-draw technique.

Sam Saguaro is living proof of the axiom "four heads are better than one."

Little Willy has a good head on his shoulders but he isn't much good with his hands.

Cousin Sara's new hat was modeled after those worn by singer Carmen Miranda.

After a very close call, Sig Saguaro was the first to volunteer for a firearms safety class.

Shelley Saguaro, shivering on a cool desert morning, discovered that wrapping herself in an ocotillo was a poor substitute for having a fur coat.

With a little persuasion, Grandpa Saguaro could be coaxed into telling tales of his participation in the Great War and how he got his Purple Heart.

Uncle Salty, again. This time his tale was something about an encounter with a large boa constrictor.

While getting quite good at balancing drinks in one hand, Sharon Saguaro began to realize that she didn't have some other necessary attributes to become a successful waitress at Hooters.

Sultan Sahara Saguaro, turban and all, was a frequent visitor from overseas.

Regular workouts at the athletic club were beginning to show results for Sue Saguaro.

Though delighted when surprised by the crew from Publishers Clearing House Sweepstakes, Shel and his wife later wished they had thrown on their bathrobes before answering the doorbell.

"Now we go a-caroling...."

The Reverend Santos Saguaro, a recent graduate of the seminary, was just getting used to wearing his clerical collar.

Uncle Sheldon giving directions to yet another lost snowbird.

"Desert Sentinels"

"Crown Jewels"

"The Guardian"

ORDER FORM
(may be copied)

Please send me more copies of *Desert Plant Personalities.*

_____ copies @$6.95   _____
Price includes Arizona State Sales Tax

Plus Postage and Handling:

1-5 copies	1.95	_____
5-10 copies	3.95	_____
More than 10 copies		No P&H charge
TOTAL REMITTED		_____

(Personal checks accepted).

Send books to:

NAME _____

STREET ADDRESS _____

CITY _____ STATE _____ ZIP _____

Send order and check to:
Mori Studio Southwest
P.O. Box 18547
Fountain Hills, AZ 85269-8547
or call us at 480-816-4407 • e-mail: morisota @aol.com